POSTAGE

≈ 0.55

F METER
8000752

A Book of Letters

Learning the ABCs has never been so much fun! Meet a circle of young friends who share good times as they pass on a chain of "letters" starting from A and going all the way to Z. Join the gang. You'll want to get your own alphabet letter chain going with your special pals!

This book is dedicated to
Luna Joksimović, a bright star
- K.W.M. & M.S.

First published in the United Kingdom in 2002 by David Bennett Books Limited,
London House, Great Eastern Wharf, Parkgate Road, London SW11 4NQ.

Text copyright ©2002 by Ken Wilson-Max.

Illustrations copyright ©2002 by Manya Stojic.

Design copyright ©2002 by Tribal Design Partnership.

ISBN 0-439-32455-6
12 11 10 9 8 7 6 5 4 3 2 1   02 03 04 05 06

Printed in China
First Scholastic Printing, April 2002

A Book of Letters

Pictures by
Manya Stojic

Story by
Ken Wilson-Max

Scholastic Inc.

New York   Toronto   London   Auckland   Sydney
Mexico City   New Delhi   Hong Kong   Buenos Aires

Bunny Bernstein decided to send
a message to her friend Christopher
Clark for Valentine's Day.

Dear Christopher,
Roses are red,
violets are blue,
the B is for me,
the C is for you.

P.S. Pass it on.

Christopher turned red when he read the note! He decided to scribble a few lines to his friend Darryl.

Christopher's note made Darryl giggle,
so he sent a letter to his pen pal on
the other side of the world.

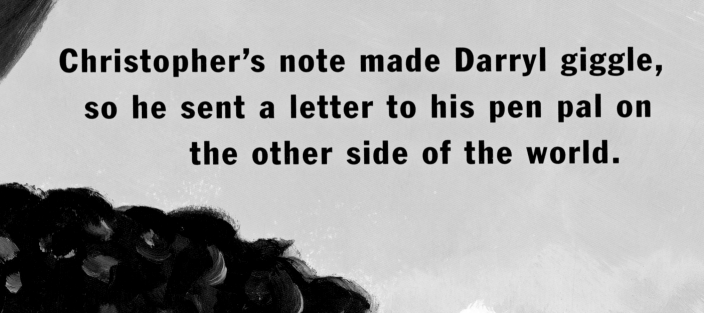

Dear Emil,
So far away.
The D is for me.
The **E** is for you.
Okay?

Love, Darryl

Send this on!

Emil opened the letter and kept
the stamps to put in his album.
Then he wrote to his friend
Ferdinand Fernandez.

Dear Ferdy,
Fancy that—
the E is for me,
the F is for
you and your cat.

Pass it on.

Georgia was very proud of her little brother's note. She thought she would write to her friend Helga Helvessen, who was going away.

Dear Helga, The G is for me. I'm going to miss you. The H is for you. Hope you'll miss me, too. keep it going!

Helga opened her letter on the plane.
She felt a little queasy.
Irma, the flight attendant,
made her feel better,
so Helga gave her
a thank-you note.

Miss Irma smiled when she read her note.
She sat down to type a letter to her
long lost cousin, Jimmy.

Keenan's dad helped him read his letter.
He wrote to Lester Lancaster,
his best friend from school,
in his best handwriting.

Lester Lancaster wore glasses that made his eyes look big. He sent a letter to his sweetheart, Margot.

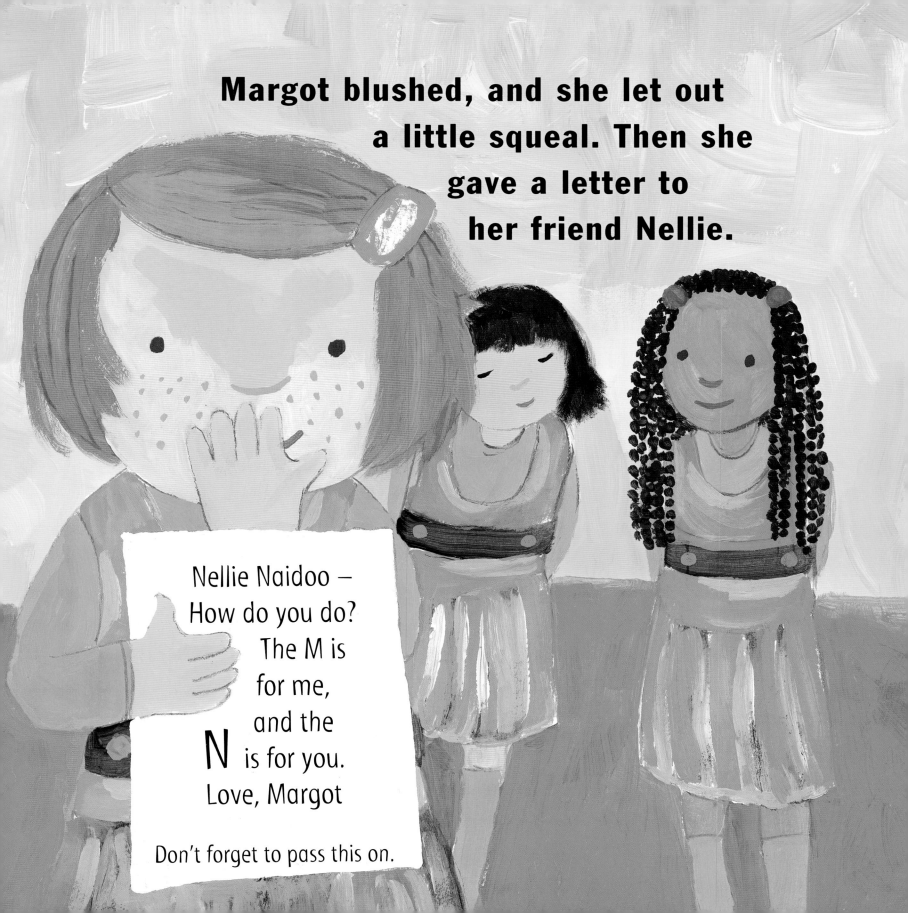

Margot blushed, and she let out a little squeal. Then she gave a letter to her friend Nellie.

Nellie Naidoo – How do you do? The M is for me, and the N is for you. Love, Margot

Don't forget to pass this on.

Nellie giggled.
She decided to write to Ozzy,
the boy from her
dance class.

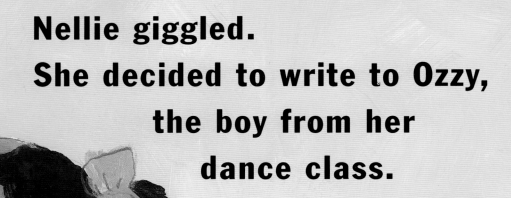

Dear Oz,
We have a class
on Friday at two.
The N is for me.

The **O** is for you.

Luv, Nellie

P.S. Pass it on.

Ozzy made a note in his diary.
Then he sent a letter
to his pen pal, Pia.

Hey Pia,

I love to dance,
and my name starts with O.
Yours starts with P,
and you love to ski!

Ozzy

Pass it on.

Pia laughed. "That silly Oz!" she thought. And she wrote a letter to her friend Quinita Quinn.

Shy Quinita Quinn
was glad to hear from Pia.
She sent a letter to her
cousin Rosie, who lived
in the desert.

Cousin Rosie
in the heat,
protect your face
and hands and feet.
A Q for me
and an **R** for you!
Love, Quinita

P.S. Pass it on, if you can.

Rosie sat in the shade
and wrote a letter to her
friend Sasha, who had just
moved away.

Dear Sasha,
The R is mine,
and the S is for you.
I hope you are fine!
Love, Rosie (and Rex,
Meow) x
P.S. Send this on
to a new friend!

Sasha was happy to hear from Rosie, and she was glad to have a reason to write to her new friend Tamara.

Dear Tammy,
A quick note from me.
My name starts with S,
and yours starts with T !
Hugs and kisses,
Sasha

P.S. Keep this going!

Tamara slurped her milk shake. She knew someone to send a letter to!

Ursula, Ursula,
We're best friends, we 2.
The T is 4 me,
and the **U** is 4 U!
Tammy xx

Pass it on.

Ursula sent a letter
to Vincent,
the boy next door!

Vinny,

Vincent at no. 23 –

and you're a

I'm a U,

V.

Pass it on.

Ursula

Vincent waved to Ursula from his window. Then he sat down to write to his best friend, Wesley.

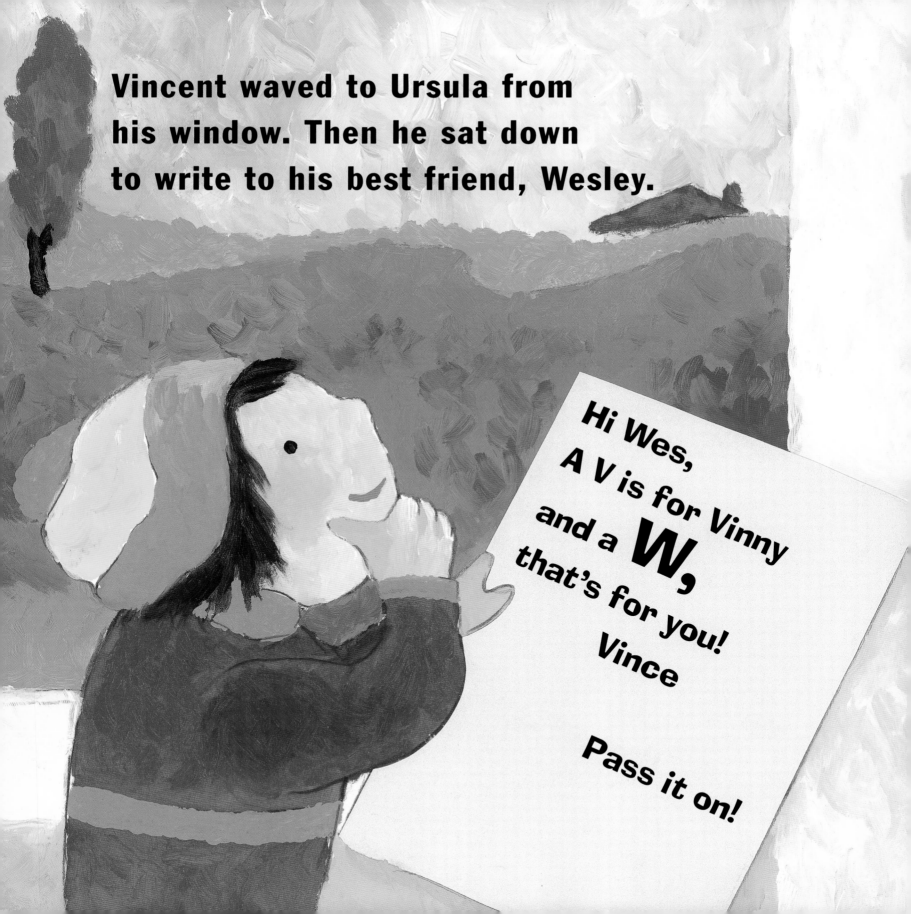

Hi Wes,
A V is for Vinny and a **W,** that's for you!
Vince

Pass it on!

Wesley had a cousin named Xavier!
He wrote to him right away.

Xavier chuckled
when he read the note.
He dropped a line
to his sister, Yvette.

Yvette was having fun at camp,
but she missed her brother, too.
She just had time to send a letter
to Zuzu, her best friend.

Dear Zuzu,
Here's something
from me to you —
a Y for me and a
Z for you, Zuzu.
Lots of love,
Yvette

And Zuzu is me! I'm going
to send Abby
a great
surprise!